everything you need to know...fast

FUNDRAISING FROM GRANTMAKERS
Trusts and Foundations

by Ruth Tovim

reviewed by Cath Cole

WIREMILL
PUBLISHING LTD

Across the world the organizations and institutions that fundraise to finance their work are referred to in many different ways. They are charities, non-profits or not-for-profit organizations, non-governmental organizations (NGOs), voluntary organizations, academic institutions, agencies, etc. For ease of reading, we have used the term Nonprofit Organization, Organization or NPO as an umbrella term throughout the *Quick*Guide series. We have also used the spellings and punctuation used by the author.

Published by
Wiremill Publishing Ltd.
Edenbridge, Kent TN8 5PS, UK
info@wiremillpublishing.com
www.wiremillpublishing.com
www.quickguidesonline.com

British Library Cataloguing in Publication Data
A catalogue record for this book is available from the British Library.

ISBN Number 1-905053-12-6

Printed by Rhythm Consolidated Berhad, Malaysia
Cover Design by Jennie de Lima and Edward Way
Design by Colin Woodman Design

CONTENTS

FUNDRAISING FROM GRANTMAKERS

TRUSTS AND FOUNDATIONS

INTRODUCTION

Unlike fundraising from individuals, which is often more of an art than a science, pursuing foundation funding can be a very manageable, orderly practice. In fact, for new organizations with innovative ideas but limited resources and few developed sources of funding, foundation funding should be a priority. Today, in the Internet Age, the process of researching, identifying and applying to foundations is easier than ever.

Despite this, too many organizations still waste valuable resources sending badly conceived proposals to inappropriate foundations which, not surprisingly, reject them. The intent of this Guide is to:

- Provide you with practical information to help you understand the grantmaking bodies called foundations and trusts.

- Help you assess whether foundation funding is suitable for the project you have in mind and what projects would be suitable for funding from foundations.

- Give you information in order to research likely foundation funders.

- Give you the best chance of making successful applications.

Foundation fundraising is not a short-term response to a funding crisis. The process of researching, writing, and waiting for a response can take months or longer. Foundation fundraising can, however, provide substantial resources for organizations and for projects that would be inappropriate for other funders.

What Is a Foundation/Trust?

A foundation (also known as a trust) is a legal, charitable entity created for the raising, holding and disbursing of funds for a charitable purpose or purposes, which can be as narrow or as broad as the founder(s) of the foundation desires and as local laws allow. Often foundations or trusts are referred to as grantmaking bodies because their disbursements are generally known as grants.

In general, a foundation will hold its capital as an endowment, making grants from the annual income earned. Depending on the foundation, grants can range from tens to millions.

Foundations may be established by a person, a family or group of people, or by a company. They are as diverse as those that fund them. Most foundations will bear the name of those that set them up, although others have names chosen to reflect their mission or giving interests.

Some foundations have been in existence for decades, have large staffs and high public profiles. Others are run from the founder's home office with the founder, the founder's family and the founder's friends all involved. In many countries, there will be specific legal requirements and tax laws relating to foundations.

TYPES OF FOUNDATIONS

Although this will vary by country, foundations generally fall into the following six types.

Family

A family foundation is a private grantmaking foundation established and funded by an individual or a family to support particular areas of interest. Family foundations may operate as the charitable chequebook of the family, with family members actively involved with the foundation and participating in the reviewing of applications for funds and grants. Other family foundations have professional staff, with the family playing little or no part in the day-to-day operations of the foundation. With older family foundations, where the original areas of interest are very broad or no longer relevant or where family members are no longer involved, grantmaking priorities have often been reinterpreted by current staff and members of the governing body.

There are two main reasons why individuals or families set up foundations:

■ Foundations are ongoing and perpetuate the family name in a way that wouldn't happen if donations were simply made by family members.

■ There are legal and tax benefits which arise when a foundation is established.

Corporate

Corporate foundations are private grantmaking organizations established by a corporation to disburse philanthropic funds. Most times they bear the name of the company and are funded on an annual basis from the income of the corporation.

Foundation funding is different from giving which is done directly from the corporation. Direct corporate giving, whether it be through sponsorship, gifts-in-kind, volunteering by staff or whatever, is often part of a marketing strategy rather than a philanthropic strategy. A separate foundation allows a company to make purely charitable grants and take advantage of charitable tax benefits, if applicable.

6 Fundraising From Grantmakers

Although a company foundation is separate from the company, the foundation will still promote the interests of the company.

Community

Community foundations are grantmaking bodies which consist of a number of funds established by individual donors. A community foundation can refer to a specific geographic community or to a community of interest (e.g., environmental). The donors' funds may be directed only to a particular nonprofit organization or cause or may be disbursed as part of the general assets of the foundation.

The advantage to donors in using a community foundation to make charitable donations is that the community foundation provides the administration and program services so that the donor need not engage staff to run his or her foundation separately. There may also be tax advantages for using a community foundation.

Government

Sometimes governments find it necessary or appropriate to establish foundations to disburse funds, such as overseas aid or lottery funds.

Special-Interest

A grantmaking organization established to raise and disburse funds for a unique purpose (e.g., medical research) is a special-interest foundation. It may be set up by a number of people or funded by the public.

Operating

An operating foundation is an arm of a charitable organization established to fund the foundation's own programs (e.g., a hospital or university foundation). The foundation usually fundraises, so in many ways it is unlike a traditional foundation; however, it may share some of the same tax and legal attributes of the traditional grantmaking body.

The structure of a foundation can vary enormously depending on its size and remit. At one end of the spectrum is an unstaffed, family foundation whose trustees meet once a year over dinner to decide what to fund, while at the other is a complex organization employing hundreds of people. The complexity of the organization is often (though not always) a reflection of the size of its endowments and annual grant giving.

The Governing Body

All foundations will have a governing body. It may be called a board of directors, board of trustees or board of governors, or something else. No matter what it's called, its mandate is to ensure that the foundation is operating legally (i.e., the endowment is safeguarded and grantmaking is in alignment with the foundation's stated purpose). If they have the authority, trustees may change or revise the foundation's funding priorities in accordance with issues they perceive as important at any given time.

With family foundations, the board may be made up entirely of family members; in the case of larger, older foundations, family representatives may make up part of the board. Community, government and special-interest foundation boards will include stakeholders such as representative community leaders and subject experts.

Many boards have direct decision-making responsibilities vis-à-vis grantmaking, although large foundations often have subcommittees of the board which serve specific functions, especially grantmaking.

Boards and subcommittees will usually have a set schedule of annual or periodic meetings at which grant applications are reviewed.

Staff

Small foundations may have one part-time or full-time staff member, often with the title of secretary, who functions as foundation administrator and grant officer. Small, special-interest foundations may have a paid expert advisor who assists with grantee selection.

Larger foundations usually have grant officers whose jobs are to manage grant applications and analyse applications for their appropriateness. These grant officers often are experts in the particular type of grants in which they work.

Foundations provide different types of grants, so it is important to understand your own funding needs as well as the types of grants provided by foundations you have identified. Different foundations may use different terminology to describe the grants they make, but the types of grants will be largely the same.

Operational

Operational or core cost grants cover various aspects of operating an organization (i.e., staffing, rent or utilities). They are often the most difficult grants to receive and the most frequently desired.

Project

This is by far the most common type of funding aimed at supporting a particular, usually time-limited project.

Capital

Grants to support capital projects such as building and renovations are extremely valuable because they can be very large and can kick-start a campaign.

Capacity-Building

A relatively recent phenomenon is the capacity-building grant, which is designed specifically to help small or new organizations become more self-sufficient in areas such as governance and fundraising.

Matching

Matching grants can only be used if the grantee raises funds from other sources which match the amount of the proposed grant. Foundations that offer matching grants do so as a method of encouraging organizations to obtain support from a range of donors.

Multiyear

Although most foundations deter organizations from becoming dependent on them for funds, some grantees (particularly those providing very specialized services) may receive a commitment for funding over a several-year period. This may be either a one-time grant that is paid over a number of years, or the foundation may agree to fund an organization or its project for several years. Either way, the amount of funding generally will be fixed.

YOUR PROJECT TO BE FUNDED

The most important aspect of seeking foundation funding has nothing to do with the foundation at all. Rather, it's about defining your own organization and the project for which you are seeking support. Being very clear about who you are and what your project is will:

- Help you identify relevant foundations (i.e., those whose funding interests, geographic scope and grant type fit your needs).

- Increase your chances of a successful application.

It is also useful to think about the types of projects that are most likely to be supported by a foundation:

- A local project will probably only attract interest from local foundations or foundations interested in your area, unless your project is new or replicable, in which case it might attract broader interest for its potential broader applicability.

- A project with a long history is unlikely to interest a foundation, while something in the planning stages may attract interest because the foundation can have input in its creation.

- Funding for building and capital projects is usually difficult to obtain.

- Funding for core costs is usually more difficult to get than funding for a project.

Once you start looking at foundations and their giving interests as described, you will start to gain experience in determining which projects are more likely than others to attract funding and to focus your foundation fundraising on those types of projects. One pitfall to avoid is creating a project to fit a funder's interests if the project is one you hadn't intended to do in any event.

When you have decided what project to seek funding for, the next step is to write a case for support. This should be completed before you even start thinking about which foundations to approach. It will ensure your thinking is clear and concise and will provide the basis for the application to the foundation.

The following is a brief description of the essential elements that should be included in your case for support.

Project Description
Summarize the project: purpose, features, time frame, who benefits.

Project Team
Describe the team members and their credentials. Include not only those who will oversee the project but also volunteers, if any, who will participate.

Project Rationale
This should be a persuasive description of why the project is important and why it should attract funding.

Budget
Make your budget as detailed as possible.

Funding Sources
List all sources of current, projected or possible funding for the project.

Background Material
Think about any further relevant information that might be used to support a later application for funding such as general information about your organization, annual reports, statistics about the sector in which your organization operates, CVs or résumés of your organization's staff and governing body, floor plans or artist renderings of proposed buildings, press clippings, letters of support.

I dentifying foundations is still a time-consuming exercise, but with the proliferation of CD-ROM and web-based directories, from both commercial and nonprofit providers, it is now easier than ever. In addition, many foundations, particularly the larger ones, now have their own websites where you can find out about their current funding priorities, grant-giving histories, guidelines and deadlines, and can download application forms.

Directories

There are many excellent foundation directories, most of which can be purchased in printed form, on CD-ROM or through online subscriptions. These services are not cheap, however; unless your organization does a lot of foundation fundraising, it would be worthwhile to check the main branches of public libraries or any umbrella groups your organization belongs to for free access to the directories.

Note that there are also some specialist directories aimed at specific sectors (e.g., the environment).

Directories can also be found through Internet search engines and online discussion groups, and by asking other organizations or contacts in the nonprofit sector.

Most of the directories are indexed by subject and geographical area, allowing you to search by both criteria. Using your case for support, establish what key words to use for a search. Remember that initially it is worthwhile to search using broad key word(s), in order to get as many results as possible.

Foundations can increasingly be found online without the need of directories. Some websites contain information about a number of foundations and can be found through search engines, nonprofit magazines, other websites, following one website to another, and so forth. Many of the foundations that will be found will have their own websites, some of which will lead to other general websites with foundation information.

Other Methods

Other ways of identifying foundations of potential interest: look online, in annual reports or in fundraising literature for funders of organizations similar to yours; ask current donors for suggestions of foundations that might be of interest; ask current foundation funders for recommendations of other foundations; or register for online discussion groups. Many fundraising organizations have specialist foundation fundraising groups; attending their meetings would be valuable not only to ask about potential foundations but also to get local advice about local foundation fundraising opportunities.

The Next Step

Once you have some results, create a list of foundations that may be interested in your organization and the project you have chosen for support. Depending on what information sources are available, entries may be extensive or minimal, but they will at least have contact information. Look at the foundation's website for information if there is one; otherwise, call or write for an information pack. What you are seeking is information about the foundation's giving interests and history, application requirements and restrictions. If it is a corporate foundation, obtain information about the company that funds it. The more information about the foundation you have, the better you can evaluate its potential interest in your project.

Carefully read the information you have obtained. Your first job is to remove any foundations from your list that are inappropriate. Pay particular attention to the following.

Giving interests – foundations will often tell you what they are interested in supporting. Some foundations will be extremely narrow in their interests (i.e., a specific disease, a particular part of the world, certain ages of children). Other foundations will give to anything that looks worthwhile or interesting to them. Crucially you are looking for a fit between your project and the giving interests of the foundation. If these don't match, you can reject that foundation no matter what else about it looks interesting.

Continues on next page

Size of grant – if you need large grants and the foundation is small and only makes small donations, it is not worth even approaching that foundation. A range of grant size may be shown in the grantmaking materials or inferred by the size of the assets of the foundation.

Deadlines – some foundations accept applications at any time throughout the year; other foundations have one or more deadlines, often several months before a grants meeting. The foundation's guidelines will help you evaluate whether the foundation will be useful for your purposes.

Geographical interest – some foundations only give locally, some give nationally, and others donate internationally. Again, you need to match your interests with the expressed interests of the foundation. However, foundations sometimes indicate that they only give in a particular geographic area when, if asked, they might be willing to consider applications for funding for a broader region. You need to evaluate whether the geographical interest is deliberately limited or whether the foundation has just never been asked from another area.

Exceptions – foundations will generally be very clear about what they DO NOT fund, i.e., capital projects or overheads. Again, this information is crucial if you are looking for funding for a capital project or for core costs. Applying for these funds when the foundation only supports projects is a waste of your and the foundation's time.

Grant-giving history – this is an excellent way to assess what a foundation is really interested in supporting, no matter what its formal guidelines say. If the foundation literature says it supports organizations across the country but its giving is largely limited to a specific area, this is valuable information. If the guidelines indicate the foundation will give grants of up to five figures but, in fact, it rarely does, you need to know that information in making your evaluation of the foundation.

Trustees/professional advisors –
it is always worth researching a foundation's board and/or advisors, because there may be links to your organization that may help you. Most foundation boards have much influence on the grantmaking process, even when a foundation has professional staff.

Some foundations have no written giving information beyond what is published in a directory. This may be because they are too small to do so, have no staff, or informally make grantmaking decisions with the founder and other board members. In some countries there is no culture of providing information to grant seekers, while in other countries there is.

If you are unable to obtain written information, it is worth trying to find out information informally by phoning the foundation office or emailing the office and/or trustees. Explain that you don't want to waste their time with an inappropriate application and are seeking information in order to ensure this.

The most important thing to understand about applying for a foundation grant is not to apply to foundations that are unsuitable. Don't waste your time or theirs.

The second most important thing to know about applying for a foundation grant is to follow the guidelines set forth by the foundation. You don't want to have your application rejected for procedural or technical reasons – you want it to be considered on the merits of the project.

Your application is your tool to convince the foundation that you are appropriate for its funding. By following the guidelines set forth for applications, you are demonstrating that you can follow the rules established by the foundation; this will provide some comfort to the foundation that you will do the same when it comes to reporting requirements as well as fulfilling the requirements of the project or program to be funded.

Your applications will vary depending on each foundation and its requirements. Treat each application with as much diligence as you would any communication to any funder. Everything matters. Your role when writing an application is to satisfy the foundation, not tell it what you feel is important.

Your application should be submitted with a covering letter signed by the head of your organization or the head of your governing body. This will show the foundation that you take the application to them seriously.

Initial Approach

Many foundations request that the first communication for funding be a brief application, usually only one or two pages. Some foundations call it a letter of inquiry, but whatever it's called, it should be prepared as carefully as a long application.

Many foundations will specify what should be included in the initial communication. Typical headings include:

- Information about your organization.
- Information about the need that the project addresses.
- Details of the project to be funded.
- Biographies of the project staff and the organization's trustees and senior staff.
- How much is being requested.
- A budget for the project.

These headings form a good template for foundations that don't have specific instructions for what the first communication should include. Communications to those foundations that do have specific instructions for grant seekers should follow the instructions given.

If you have identified any trustees with links to your organization, try to contact them and let them know you will be submitting a letter of inquiry, an application or other communication. They may ask that it be sent to them so they can submit it on your behalf, or they may be willing to write a letter to accompany it.

Reviewer's Comment
It is worth emphasizing the length of time it can take from the submission of an initial application or expression of interest until the trust or foundation actually makes a decision. This can often be the most frustrating part of fundraising from foundations and should be seriously considered by anyone starting to work in this area. It is definitely not a "quick win" style of fundraising, especially if you are looking for larger sums.

The Funding Proposal
If the foundation has received your letter of inquiry or first communication and wants to know more about you and the program, it will provide you with either an application form or guidelines on what the application should contain. And

Continues on next page

some foundations will require a full application as the first or only communication. If the foundation has provided instructions for an application, follow them! Some foundations receive hundreds of worthy applications, and not following their rules may disqualify you before the merits of the project have a chance to be considered.

In terms of content, if you have done a thorough job of making your case for support, usually you must simply adapt the information to fit the foundation's required format. Having said that, always pay careful attention to specific requests like budget breakdowns and other measurable criteria.

Be especially careful if you are applying for one aspect of a project (i.e., funds for an event or a publication). You can send the whole case for support, but make sure what you are applying for is clear and that your budget corresponds to it.

HINTS

Some hints for preparing a letter of inquiry, short application (one to two pages) or full application:

- Follow instructions!

- If the foundation request is for two pages, ensure you write succinctly. Don't squeeze ten pages into two by using small typefaces and small margins.

- Use the headings requested by the foundation and fill in the information under each heading. This ensures you have answered all the questions and helps the person checking the application as well.

- Don't send anything that isn't requested. It won't help.

- Do send everything that is requested.

- If you don't understand the meaning of something in the application guidelines, ask. The worst that can happen? The foundation isn't helpful. The best that can happen? You are remembered as being particularly eager to meet the requirements.

- Applying to a foundation is about matching your project to their interests. Show them how your project does so. Save the emotive language for letters to individual donors.

- Ensure you meet all deadlines.

- Don't bend the truth or omit significant information in your application. If there are problems, say so. You want to build a relationship as well as receive a grant.

- Remember that luck often plays a part in achieving a positive response.

Be prepared for a negative response. Foundations receive many more proposals than they can possibly fund. The usual response will be a polite letter, which will not give you much insight into why your application was rejected. Sometimes you will hear nothing from the foundation at all, which is particularly frustrating but not uncommon.

Consider asking the foundation for feedback on why your proposal was rejected. It will help you with future foundation applications and maybe even with this particular foundation.

Don't be disappointed with a rejection and don't feel you can't make another application to the foundation unless you discover that the foundation does not fund the type of project for which you are seeking support.

Reviewer's Comment
The impact of world events on trust fundraising cannot be overstated. Funding from trusts and foundations is generally dependent on income from their investments. When income is reduced, the size and number of grants given out are reduced and, thus, the market is more competitive than ever.

It's always great to get a grant, and the first one can be very satisfying. The job now is to ensure you meet any conditions imposed with the grant. Take note of what is required and comply. Typical requirements that might be imposed are as follows.

Reports – the foundation will probably provide you with particular grant requirements that you must report back on, usually annually but sometimes more often.

It is important that your organization establish from the beginning who is responsible for the reports (for example, the project leader or the fundraiser), ensure that the report deadlines are appropriately noted and the reports are prepared and sent on time. Not only does this give you an opportunity to show the excellence of your project but this also allows you to demonstrate that you will fulfill expectations, a very positive step toward receiving a future grant.

Grant tracking – you may be required to provide details of the grant's use; in some cases, very detailed reports will be required. If this is a condition of your grant, you will need to establish a separate line item for it so you can report on how the grant was used. This is particularly important if the grant was designated for a specific activity.

Recognition – ask the foundation how it likes to be recognized. Unlike individual donors, foundations are usually not concerned about recognition. However, most foundations appreciate acknowledgment on websites, in annual reports, in newsletters, etc., and will be happy to provide you with their logos for publication purposes.

Visits – invite trustees and staff to visit your project, facilities and special events when appropriate.

Timely, businesslike reporting and appropriate recognition will go a long way toward establishing your organization as a trustworthy grantee.

Although it is not usually a sustainable strategy to become dependent on a particular foundation for a particular resource stream, some foundations will provide multiyear grants to organizations or develop ongoing relationships with organizations that they believe are providing an important service in their area of interest.

Reviewer's Comment

I feel more positively about multiyear grants. Longer-term grants can create a great element of sustainability for an organization, and I have found that some foundations prefer to support (and work in partnership with) a number of selected nonprofits for a longer period of time, rather than spread their support around. This way, they are still around when the longer-term benefits of their grants are finally seen.

In addition, staff members from different foundations often know one another. They talk. They share information. This is particularly so with foundations giving to the same types of projects, geographical areas or nonprofit sectors. If you have been a good grantee, your chance of receiving a grant from another foundation may be enhanced or at least not damaged. If you have been a problem, it is highly likely that the information will be shared and your chances seriously diminished.

Remember, also, that trustees are individuals. Even if the foundation is unable to support the same grantee on a continual basis, it does no harm to secure the commitment and goodwill of individual trustees.

FINAL THOUGHTS

The key to successful fundraising from foundations can be summarized as the three R's:

Research – investigating potential trusts and the particular criteria and requirements of those on your shortlist.

Relevance – selecting an appropriate project for the right foundation, and including relevant and well-targeted information in the application process.

Reporting – providing reports as requested to ensure a professional image is maintained at all times and to assure future goodwill toward your organization.

RUTH TOVIM

Ruth Tovim, currently Acting Director of Development at City University, London, has dedicated the last ten years to fundraising for a variety of organizations in the sectors of international development, health, environment, and higher education in Canada and the UK.

Ruth has also worked as an independent consultant in Canada and the United States, assisting grass-roots organizations to build and expand their fundraising capacity. Her expertise includes development audits; prospect research; setting up trusts; setting up annual-giving, workplace-giving and major-gift programs; and board development.

Ruth has a BA in History from Concordia University, Montreal. She is an Israeli-born Canadian citizen.

Cath Cole, Reviewer

Cath Cole is the Head of Corporate and Trust Fundraising at Terrence Higgins Trust, UK, where she has worked since February 2002. She manages a staff of four, who raise funds from trusts and foundations, the Lottery Fund, and a wide range of EU and nonstatutory funders. She also manages corporate fundraising.

Cath has worked in the UK charity sector for five years. Before Terrence Higgins Trust, she was the Senior Corporate Account Director at The Children's Society, and prior to that she worked as Corporate Account Manager at Children Nationwide (now the Wellchild Trust).

She came to the nonprofit sector after working for Dixons Stores Group and travelling for two years around Asia, Australasia and North America.